CU08736828

CARGOES

[signature]

HMS *Queen* at Mudros, by Kenneth D Shoesmith 1918
'Mudros in itself offered nothing to the Allied fleets but a
safe anchorage.'
From *Gallipoli* by John Masefield

CARGOES

A Celebration of the Sea Through the Pen and the Paintbrush of
John Masefield
&
Kenneth D Shoesmith
Compiled and Edited by Glyn L Evans
with the permission of the Estate of John Masefield

Published by Saron Publishers 2019

Copyright © Glyn L Evans 2019
Copyright © John Masefield 2019
All rights reserved

No part of this publication may be reproduced, stored in a
retrieval system, or transmitted, in any form or by any means,
without the prior permission in writing of the publisher, nor
be otherwise circulated in any form of binding or cover other
than that in which it is published and without a similar
condition including this condition being imposed on the
subsequent purchaser

The poems of John Masefield are reproduced by kind
permission of the Society of Authors
The Estate of John Masefield

A catalogue record for this book is available from the
British Library

ISBN-13: 978 1 913297 01 5

Saron Publishers
Pwllmeyrick House
Mamhilad
Mon
NP4 8RG

www.saronpublishers.co.uk

info@saronpublishers.co.uk

Follow us on Facebook and Twitter

Printed and bound in the UK

DEDICATION

This book is dedicated to the memory of my late father, William Arthur Evans, a former pupil of the Birkenhead Institute. His prize upon matriculation in 1931, awarded by the then Head Master, E Wynne-Jones, was a copy of *The Collected Poems of John Masefield*. The book, now showing its age somewhat, sits beside me as I write; a tangible reminder of a joy once shared.

A learned person always has riches within hinself.

Contents

CARGOES

Foreword
by Captain Richard Woodman LVO
Elder Brother, Trinity House

Poets Laureate come and go; the lives of poster-artists are even more ephemeral, yet both occupations have impact, even immediacy. While regard for such achievements goes in and – mostly - out of fashion, it may be argued that it is important that neglect does not consign the significance of some of these worthies to complete oblivion.

The present national disregard for matters maritime is, in the eyes of some few of us, not merely a subject for regret, but the core of a lesson from history that we ignore at our peril and Glyn L Evans is to be warmly congratulated in the gentle reminder of all this which is presented in this charming book. Of the two aspects of our maritime heritage that we have almost entirely lost sight of, the mercantile rather than the naval is that which receives most emphasis in this synthesis of the work of the poet John Masefield and the artist Kenneth Shoesmith.

Both were Old Boys of the static training-ship *Conway,* once moored in the River Mersey, and both went to sea. Masefield, a victim of chronic sea-sickness, did not stay, but his enforced exile from his chosen profession lent a power to his evocation of the sea-life in verse. Shoesmith became a Chief Officer with the Royal Mail Line before taking to commercial art. Masefield's *Sea Fever* is still remembered, and Shoesmith's formal art is still extant aboard the RMS *Queen Mary* at Long Beach, California, but neither man occupies any real place in the modern pantheon of our national 'greats'. Yet the vocations of both derived from a deep understanding and appreciation of our national significance as a maritime country, to say nothing of our national dependence upon sea-transport and sea-trade.

While Masefield's sea verse can be dismissed lightly as too romantic to reflect reality, this is an opinion open to argument. While merchant and naval jack was a pragmatic fellow, generally dismissive of such flummeries, he was not indifferent to his own life being accorded the status and dignity it deserved in the national consciousness. Masefield sought to accomplish this.

Jack Tar was even more aware of the veracity of Shoesmith's labours, for the man I have somewhat disparaged as a 'poster-artist' was rather more than that. True, his bold and vivid style does not lack that eye-catching vivacity so essential to commercial intent, but it is also utterly faithful to its subject. Few seafarers can criticise Shoesmith's work and, where ships are concerned, seafaring opinion is unforgiving.

Both Masefield and Shoesmith were members of the Seven Seas Club which, in their day, was entirely composed of men who had served at sea and both knew the sea-life and the watery world from the inside. This knowledge and understanding runs through their work, giving it an integrity which makes this complementary combination of their output all the more exciting and vibrant. Their individual contemplation of the maritime scene of their day is thoroughly sound, even though today it has about it the *tritesse* of nostalgia. All this, this book tells us, is something we have lost.

But there is also an appeal – very much of the artists' time – to contemporary interest in Tudor seafaring, even piratical exploits. These add colour to the pages that follow, for while this is a book containing a serious message, it is also a book to savour and enjoy, a delight to the eye and ear as much as the intellect. Glyn Evans is to be congratulated in bringing the almost forgotten work of these two talented men together, reminding us of who we are, where we have come from and what – in the past – we did to earn our place in the world.

Richard Woodman
Harwich 2017

Samuel Pepys, Diarist and Secretary to the Admiralty, at the Royal Dockyard, Deptford

One of Shoesmith's paintings on board RMS
Queen Mary

CARGOES
Introduction

Synergy has been defined as 'the cooperation of multiple elements to produce a result greater than the sum of their individual efforts'. One might also add 'an over-used word, much beloved by newly-appointed CEOs, and an essential part of any self-respecting corporate entity's mission statement'. Cynicism aside, there are times when two plus two does seem to make five and perhaps never more so than in the entertainment world where the collaborations of Gilbert & Sullivan *(The Mikado)*, Lerner & Loewe *(My Fair Lady)*, and Rodgers & Hammerstein *(South Pacific)* eclipsed their individual achievements.

Examples from film and television include partnerships such as those of Laurel & Hardy and Morecambe & Wise, each individual a comic in his own right but more than doubly funny as a double act. Fewer examples exist in the world of books, although the collaboration of Basil Lubbock and Jack Spurling, writer and marine artist respectively, *(The Best of Sail)* with a shared experience of life aboard clipper ships (both survived a fall from their ship's rigging), is an exception.

The opportunity for a similar collaboration that so nearly came about involved the poet and prose writer, John Masefield and the maritime artist and poster designer, Kenneth D Shoesmith. While there is no evidence to suggest that a collaboration was considered on a grand scale by these two, we do have a tantalising glimpse of what might have been, in the form of Shoesmith's dust jacket illustrations for several of Masefield's books including *The Bird of Dawning* and *Victorious Troy*. Although both men had been cadets in HMS *Conway,* there was a ten year gap between their terms on board.

This gap came during that transitional period when the great grain ships on the Australia run and the graceful clippers of the China tea trade shared the high seas with salt-caked smoke-stacked steamers. Nevertheless, it was to be a *Conway* connection that put them in touch each with the other. In 1922, the retired Captain Superintendent of HMS *Conway,* Captain W H Broadbent, founded the Seven Seas Club as a focal point of social contact for former *Conway* cadets with time on their hands when in London. Masefield and Shoesmith were among the first to join and I am pleased to report that the Seven Seas Club continues to flourish today.

When a poet or artist is able to truly capture, in words or pictures, man's fight for mastery of the sea, he may be counted by those who fully appreciate these two art forms, a master of his craft. The honours conferred upon Masefield (Order of Merit) and Shoesmith (Member of the Royal Institute of Painters in Water Colour) speak for themselves. This book sets out to examine how such a collaboration between these two masters of their craft might have flourished, and to envisage the finished article.

'...Homeward bound down New York Harbour...'

A Steerage Steward

A few years ago I was in New York City trying to get a passage home aboard some liner, or freight or cattle steamer. I had a little money in my pocket – just enough, in fact, to pay for a steerage ticket to Liverpool; but I preferred to work my way, so that I might not be destitute when I stepped ashore, as I should have been had I taken a berth. It was the Fourth of July when I started my quest. The weather was extremely hot, and my frequent repulses were depressing.

Presently I went aboard one of the big liners and got into talk with the man on the gangway. He told me to pass in boldly, and put a good face on it and ask to see the captain. Cheek was the main thing, he said, and if the captain didn't kick me overboard, he would surely give me a passage. So I passed aboard, called a steward and sent him to the captain to say that I wished to see him. The captain very politely returned answer that he was engaged at the moment but that he would wait upon me immediately, so would I mind taking a seat? I took a seat. Bye and bye the captain came to me and heard my request, and seemed much amused at my cheek in sending for him. Then he sent a minion for the head of the steerage stewards, who came hurriedly, brushing the dust from his jacket.

The captain asked him if he were short of a hand. The steward said he was. The captain said that I was to have the vacancy, and that he hoped that one of the other stewards would lend me a cap and an apron for the passage, I signed the ship's articles, got my gear aboard, borrowed a cap and apron and began my duties. Less than half an hour later the ship's bell was beaten, the gangways were run in and the ship was homeward bound down New York Harbour. My first job was to assist in the mustering of the steerage passengers at the general collection of tickets.

'A tall ship and a star to steer her by...'

Sea Fever

I must go down to the sea again, to the lonely sea and the sky,
And all I ask is a tall ship and a star to steer her by,
And the wheel's kick and the wind's song and the white sail's shaking,
And a grey mist on the sea's face and a grey dawn breaking.

I must down to the seas again, for the call of the running tide
Is a wild call and a clear call that may not be denied;
And all I ask is a windy day with the white clouds flying,
And the flung spray and the blown spume, and the sea-gulls crying.

I must down to the seas again, to the vagrant gypsy life,
To the gull's way and the whale's way where the wind's like a whetted knife;
And all I ask is a merry yarn from a laughing fellow-rover,
And a quiet sleep and a sweet dream when the long trick's over.

'...his great delight and interest was the painting of sailing ships...'

The *Bird of Dawning*
or
The Fortune of the Sea

Nearly seventy years ago, Cruiser Trewsbury, the second mate of the homeward-bound China clipper, *Blackgauntlet,* was keeping the first watch in a September evening in the extremest Northern verge of the North East Trades. His Christian name was Cyril, but he had been nicknamed 'Cruiser' while on the *Conway,* and the name had followed him about the seas. He was a compact, forceful young man of nearly twenty-two, in his seventh year at sea. He was an excellent sailor and shipmate; he had a fairly good tenor voice; he had made it a rule to learn a new language on each round voyage; and had written but not published a little manual on Compass Deviation. But his great delight and interest was the painting of sailing ships in all possible positions and situations. His ambition was to 'pass for Master' on his return to England, give up the sea, go to an art school in Paris and become a painter.

All through the Roaring Forties and the South East Trades their luck had held: they had gone their best, with a never-failing power of wind behind them. Well into the North East Trades, they had felt that they were breaking all records ever known in the passage, and that the miracle of their luck might well be theirs only. Then, unaccountably, and in a way not known before by any man on board, the North East Trades had failed them. They had died away into nothing, and had left them for a miserable week, expecting but not finding the Westerlies that should have been bowling them home into the Channel. It had been like a week in the Doldrums, with hot weather, light airs, and occasional violent squalls. Day after day, watch after watch, they had felt their chance of a record passage and of the London Prize die away.

'Ships and the sea; there's nothing finer made.'

Dauber (A)

He was the painter in that swift ship's crew –
Lampman and painter – tall, a slight-built man,
Young for his years, and not yet twenty-two;
Sickly, and not yet brown with the sea's tan.
Bullied and damned at since the voyage began,
'Being neither man nor seaman by his tally,'
He bunked with the idlers just abaft the galley.

Si talked with Dauber, standing by the side.
'Why did you come to sea, painter?' he said.
'I want to be a painter,' he replied,
'And know the sea and ships from A to Z,
And paint great ships at sea before I'm dead;
Ships under skysails running down the Trade –
Ships and the sea; there's nothing finer made.'

'But there's so much to learn, with sails and ropes,
And how the sails look, full or being furled,
And how the lights change in the troughs and slopes,
And the sea's colours up and down the world,
And how a storm looks when the sprays are hurled
High as the yard (they say) I want to see;
There's none ashore can teach such things to me.'

'It's not been done, the sea, not yet been done,
From the inside, by one who really knows;
I'd give up all if I could be the one,
But art comes dear the way the money goes.
So I have come to sea, and I suppose
Three years will teach me all I want to learn
And make enough to keep me till I earn.'

'That leap and light,
and sudden change to green,'

Dauber (B)

Even as he spoke his busy pencil moved,
Drawing the leap of water off the side
Where the great clipper trampled iron-hooved,
Making the blue hills of the sea divide,
Shearing a glittering scatter in her stride,
And leaping on full tilt with all sails drawing,
Proud as a war-horse, snuffing battle, pawing.

'I cannot get it yet – not yet,' he said;
'That leap and light, and sudden change to green,
And all the glittering from the sunset's red,
And the milky colours where the bursts have been,
And then the clipper striding like a queen
Over it all, all beauty to the crown.
I see it all, I cannot put it down.

'It's hard not to be able. There, look there!
I cannot get the movement nor the light;
Sometimes it almost makes a man despair
To try and try and never get it right.
Oh, if I could – oh, if I only might,
I wouldn't mind what hells I'd have to pass,
Not if the whole world called me fool and ass.'

'Here you are taught Sea Truth'

The *Conway*

Part 1

The *Conway's* word to the new-comer

Here you will put off childhood and be free
Of England's oldest guild: here your right hand
Is the Ship's right, for service at command;
Your left may save your carcase from the sea.
Here you will leap to orders instantly
And murmur afterwards, when you disband.
Here you will polish brass and scrub with sand,
And know as little leisure as the bee.

Here you are taught Sea Truth, to eat hard bread,
To suffer with a rigid upper lip,
And live by Look-Out, Latitude and Lead.

Here you are linked with Sailors, who abide
The tempest and the turning of the tide,
Disaster and the sinking of the ship.

'Butting through the channel......'

Cargoes

Quinquireme of Nineveh from distant Ophir
Rowing home to haven in sunny Palestine,
With a cargo of ivory,
And apes and peacocks,
Sandlewood, cedarwood and sweet white wine.

Stately Spanish galleon coming from the Isthmus,
Dipping through the Tropics by the palm-green shores,
With a cargo of diamonds,
Emeralds, amethysts,
Topazes, and cinnamon, and gold moidores.

Dirty British coaster with a salt-caked smoke stack
Butting through the Channel in the mad March days,
With a cargo of Tyne coal,
Road-rail, pig-lead,
Firewood, iron-ware, and cheap tin trays.

'...a sunny pleasant anchorage...'

Port Of Many Ships

It's a sunny pleasant anchorage, is Kingdom Come,
Where crews is always layin' aft for double-tots o' rum,
'N' there's dancin' 'n' fiddlin' of ev'ry kind o' sort,
It's a fine place for sailor-men is that there port.
 'N' I wish –
 I wish as I was there.

The wind is never nothin' more than jest light airs,
'N' no-one gets belayin'-pinned, 'n' no-one never swears,
Yer free to loaf an' laze around, yer pipe atween yer lips,
Lollin' on the fo'c's'le, sonny, lookin' at the ships.
 'N' I wish –
 I wish as I was there.

For ridin' in the anchorage the ships of all the world
Have got one anchor down 'n' all sails furled.
All the sunken hookers 'n' the crews as took 'n' died
They lays there merry, sonny, swingin' to the tide.
 'N' I wish –
 I wish as I was there.'

Drowned old wooden hookers green wi' drippin' wrack,
Ships as never fetched to port, as never came back,
Swingin' to the blushin' tide, dippin' to the swell,
'N' the crews all singin', sonny, beatin' on the bell,
 'N' I wish –
 I wish as I was there.

'Unrecognised, you put us in your debt...'

For All Seafarers

Even in peace, scant quiet is at sea;
In war, each revolution of the screw,
Each breath of air that blows the colours free,
May be the last life movement known to you.

Death, thrusting up or down, may disunite
Spirit from body, purpose from the hull,
With thunder, bringing leaving of the light,
With lightning letting nothingness annul.

No rock, no danger, bears a warning sign,
No lighthouse scatters welcome through the dark;
Above the sea, the bomb; afloat the mine;
Beneath, the gangs of the torpedo-shark.

Year after year, with insufficient guard,
Often with none, you have adventured thus;
Some, reaching harbour, maimed and battle-scarred,
Some, never more returning, lost to us.

But, if you 'scape, tomorrow, you will steer
To peril once again, to bring us bread,
To dare again, beneath the sky of fear,
The moon-moved graveyard of your brothers dead.

Unrecognized, you put us in your debt;
Unthanked, you enter, or escape, the grave;
Whether your land remember or forget
You saved the land, or died to try to save.

'You swept across the waters like a Queen...'

The *Wanderer*

You swept across the waters like a Queen,
Finding a path where never trackway showed,
Daylong you coultered the ungarnered clean
Casting your travelling shadow as you strode.

And in the nights, when lamps were lit, you sped
With gleams running bedside you, like to hounds,
Swift, swift, a dappled glitter of light shed
On snatching sprays above collapsing mounds.

And after many a calm and many a storm,
Nearing the land, your sailors saw arise
The pinnacles of snow where streamers form,
And the ever-dying surf that never dies.

Then, laden with Earth's spoils, you used to come
Back, from the ocean's beauty to the roar
Of all the hammers of the mills of home,
Your wandering sailors dragged you to the shore,

Singing, to leave you muted and inert,
A moping place for seagulls in the rain
While city strangers trod you with their dirt,
And landsmen loaded you for sea again.

'...every space held mercy for the hurt,'

The Ambulance Ship
Port of London Authority. A Morning Drill

Now, under War, another order shewed:
The noble bareness to which seamen strip
The work- and living-quarters of a ship,
Was made a ring, for battling death and dirt.
Now, every space held mercy for the hurt,
That cleanliness and hope might come to grip
With every devil loosed from hell's abode.

In light and spotlessness the beds were ranged,
The stretchers were prepared, the windows freed
To pass the wounded through in case of need;
The hempen slings lay ready on the deck
For lifting bodies round protruding wreck;
To each imagined ill, forethoughtful heed,
Sea discipline by loving kindness changed.

There stood the men and women of the crew.
Would that I had their portraits painted here,
Those faces of devotion, courage, cheer,
Each, in its way, an image of our best,
Each, always, daily making someone blest
By bringing hope and putting away fear
And shining out with life when murder flew.

'...like a tarry Buccaneer...'

The Tarry Buccaneer

I'm going to be a pirate with a bright brass pivot-gun,
And an island in the Spanish Main beyond the setting sun,
And a silver flagon full of red wine to drink when work is done,
Like a fine old salt-sea scavenger, like a tarry Buccaneer.

With a sandy creek to careen in, and a pig-tailed Spanish mate,
And under my main-hatches a sparkling merry freight
Of doubloons and double moidores and pieces of eight,
Like a fine old salt-sea scavenger, like a tarry Buccaneer.

With a taste for Spanish wine-shops and for spending my doubloons,
And a crew of swart mulattoes and black-eyed octoroons,
And a thoughtful way with mutineers of making them maroons,
Like a fine old salt-sea scavenger, like a tarry Buccaneer.

With a sash of crimson velvet and a diamond-hilted sword,
And a silver whistle about my neck secured to a golden cord,
And a habit of taking captives and walking them along a board,
Like a fine old salt-sea scavenger, like a tarry Buccaneer.

With a spy-glass tucked beneath my arm and a cocked hat cocked askew,
And a long low rakish schooner a-cutting of the waves in two,
And a flag of skull and cross-bones the wickedest the ever flew,
Like a fine old salt-sea scavenger, like a tarry Buccaneer.

'Rowing was the chief interest and topic
of conversation.'

The *Conway*

Rowing

Rowing was a daily or almost daily duty to anyone of average stature. The ship then carried two ten-oared cutters, one four-oared cutter, one dinghy, one jolly-boat, one sixteen-oared barge and two six-oared racing gigs.

Four at least of these boats were in the water every day, some of them with fixed crews, some passing for the day from one top to another. Rowing was the chief interest and topic of conversation. Each man knew to a hair the merits of every other man as an oar, and the place he should occupy in an ideal crew.

Throughout the summer and early autumn the tops and watches raced each other once or twice a week. Special crews were picked to race each other, now in one cutter now in another. At the beginning of every term two special cutters' crews were picked for the first and last run of the day. These crews were known as the morning and evening cutters. They contained among them the twenty best oars in the ship, and from those twenty the racing gigs' crew were picked.

The style taught was what we called the *Conway* style. It was a style well adapted for the Mersey, where the tides are often exceedingly swift and the water rough. Any good crew was eagerly watched and encouraged. When the morning and evening cutters had pulled together for a fortnight, their runs were followed by all hands, and every beauty and blemish was noticed and discussed.

'...running rather wild before a
lumping, following sea...'

Victorious Troy or the *Hurrying Angel*

It was a wild afternoon in the South Pacific in the late summer (late February there) of 1922. The full-rigged ship, the *Hurrying Angel,* was running uneasily, under reduced canvas, homeward bound with grain from Melbourne. Away astern and on her starboard quarter, to the north and east, the sky was dirty and dark, livid above the darkness, and plumey above the glare, with angry whitish manes and smudges swiftly changing. The wind was freshening with squalls of rain; the sea was rising, somewhat confusedly; the sun, such as he was, now about to die in an evil heaven, was a sightless eye of paleness surrounded by a halo. In the air there was some quality beside that of menace which warred upon the body and the soul, giving to one an irritable touchiness and to the other a sense of dread.

To Dick Pomfret, the senior apprentice, who was at the wheel, this sense of dread had come before, more than once, as a storm signal. He put it down to some effect of changing atmospheric pressure on the skin and took it to be a useful warning. He had been nearly two years in the *Hurrying Angel;* he had steered her throughout that time, taking his regular trick, in fair weather and foul.

He had often seen her like this, running rather wild, before a lumping, following sea, snarling, whining and complaining, putting her snout down into it, then rising, dripping, and shearing on again, with the sea white from her passing. She was now doing nine; she had done eleven and twelve earlier in the day, but they had shortened her down when the Mate's watch came on deck at noon. It was plain to all hands she had too much on her, but they understood her Captain's wish to drive her. It was the first plentiful fair wind after weeks of failing Trades, calms and light airs. They were in what the newspapers called the Grain Race.

'The lights of steamers passing to the sea.'

The *Conway*

Part II

After forty years

Let us walk round: the night is dark but fine,
And from the fo'c's'le we shall surely see
The lights of steamers passing to the sea,
And all the city lamp-light, line on line.

There on the flood the trampled trackways shine
With hasting gleamings shaken constantly,
The River is the thing it used to be
Unchanged, unlike those merry mates of mine.

This is the very deck, the wind that blows
Whines in the self-same rigging: surely soon
Eight bells will strike, and to his fading tune
Will come the supper-call from Wally Blair:
And then alive, from all the graves none knows,
Will come the boys we knew, the boys we were.

'...Mouths were make for tankards...'

Captain Stratton's Fancy

Oh some are fond of red wine, and some are fond of white,
And some are fond of dancing by the pale moonlight;
But rum alone's the tipple, and the heart's delight
  Of the old bold mate of Henry Morgan.

Oh some are fond of Spanish wine, and some are fond of French,
And some'll swallow tay and stuff fit only for a wench;
But I'm for right Jamaica till I roll beneath the bench,
  Says the old bold mate of Henry Morgan.

Oh some are fond of fiddles, and a song well sung,
And some are all for music for to lilt upon the tongue;
But mouths were made for tankards, and sucking at the bung,
  Says the old bold mate of Henry Morgan.

Oh some are fond of dancing, and some are fond of dice,
And some are all for red lips, and pretty lasses' eyes;
But a right Jamaica puncheon is a finer prize
  To the old bold mate of Henry Morgan.

Oh some are sad and wretched folk that go in silken suits,
And there's a mort of wicked rogues that live in good reputes;
So I'm all for drinking honestly, and dying in my boots,
  Like an old bold mate of Henry Morgan.

'There in the Sloyne,
abreast Rock Ferry pier...'

1959 - HMS *Conway*'s Centenary Year

A hundred years ago, when ships were wood
And rigging hemp, this ship of ours began
With hope (man's best begetter of all good)
For England's props, the ship and sailor man.

There in the Sloyne, abreast Rock Ferry pier
This August day began the thing desired
The *'Conway'* (with her future lying near)
The words of hope were uttered, hearts were fired.

Relics of those old 'ships' are with us still
Some of the hope has been achieved, but more
Waits for the living *'Conways'* to fulfil
In all the seas that ring this planet's shore.

Up with her *'Conways'* all; abandon fears,
Let us do better this next hundred years.

'It's pleasant in Holy Mary
By San Marie Lagoon,'

St Mary's Bells

It's pleasant in Holy Mary
By San Marie Lagoon,
The bells they chime and jingle
From dawn to afternoon.
They rhyme and chime and mingle,
They pulse and boom and beat,
And the laughing bells are gentle
And the mournful bells are sweet.

Oh, who are the men that ring them,
The bells of San Marie,
Oh, who but sonsie* seamen
Come in from over sea,
And merrily in the belfries
They rock and sway and hale,
And sends the bells a-jangle,
And down the lusty ale

It's pleasant in Holy Mary
To hear the beaten bells
Come booming into music,
Which throbs, and clangs and swells,
From sunset till the daybreak,
From dawn to afternoon.
In the port of Holy Mary
On San Marie Lagoon.

* Robust and comely with a suggestion of 'lucky'.

'They dare all weathers...'

For The Men of The Merchant Navy and Fishing Fleets

They dare all weathers in all climes and seas
In every kind of ship; the risks they run
Are all the greatest underneath the sun.
Their Fortune is as flinty as their bread.

Some truces Nature grants them, never peace;
The work they do is hourly undone.
By them, we make our money and are fed,
Let England, doing Justice, honour these.

'We'll be clear of the Channel...'

A Valediction

We're bound for blue water where the great winds blow,
It's time to get the tacks aboard, time for us to go;
The crowd's at the capstan and the tune's in the shout,
'A long pull, a strong pull, *and warp the hooker out.*'

The bow-wash is eddying, spreading from the bows,
Aloft and loose the topsails and someone give a rouse
A salt Atlantic chanty shall be music to the dead,
'A long pull, a strong pull, *and the yard to the masthead.*'

Green and merry run the seas, the wind comes cold,
Salt and strong and pleasant, and worth a mint of gold;
And she's staggering, swooping, as she feels her feet,
'A long pull, a strong pull, *and aft the main-sheet.*'

Shrilly squeal the running sheaves, the weather-gear strains,
Such a clatter of chain-sheets, the devil's in the chains;
Over us the bright stars, under us the drowned,
'A long pull, a strong pull, *and we're outward bound.*'

Yonder, round and ruddy is the mellow old moon,
The red-funnelled tug has gone, and now, sonny, soon
We'll be clear of the Channel, so watch how you steer,
'Ease her when she pitches, *and so-long, my dear.*'

'...to help the work at capstan...'

The Seven Seas Shanty Book

'This book of Shanties is the outcome of a desire on the part of the members of the Seven Seas Club (mainly composed of past and present officers of the Merchant Service) to have the singing of Sea Shanties as an integral part of the programme at their monthly Dinners.' So wrote John Sampson, author of the book upon its publication in 1926, four years after the Club's foundation. In his foreword to the book, John Masefield wrote:

'The tunes of these songs have been adapted by the sailors of many generations from many sources. Some are old English ballad airs, others seem to have been taken from the tunes of popular hymns, from dance-music or music-hall songs and from the working songs of negroes. They were used by the men of the Merchant Service to help the work at capstans, halliards, sheets, tacks, bowlines, other gear and pumps. It is perhaps impossible for anyone who has not had the privilege of hearing them sung under the conditions for which they were made, to realise how much they helped the work. It used to be said that "a song was ten men on the rope". This was not an exaggeration. Every sailor must have seen men failing to do a piece of work without a song, yet doing it with pleasure and ease with the song to help them.

Part of the value of the songs, no doubt, was in the timing of the haul, but the great results achieved by them came from the excitement and zest which the singing gave to the task. It often seemed as though new life entered the singers as they sang. Perhaps nobody ever heard one of these songs being sung at the rope or capstan without feeling that song was indeed a divine thing and a gift of gods to men.'

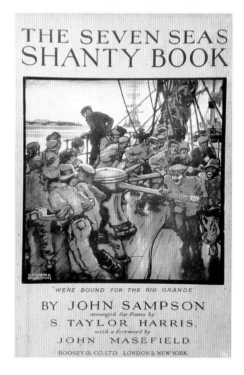

THE SEVEN SEAS SHANTY BOOK

"WE'RE BOUND FOR THE RIO GRANDE"

BY JOHN SAMPSON
arranged for Piano by
S. TAYLOR HARRIS,
with a foreword by
JOHN MASEFIELD.
BOOSEY & CO.LTD. LONDON & NEW YORK

'Ship after ship, crammed with soldiers'

Gallipoli

The transports (all painted black) lay in tiers, well within the harbour, the men of war nearer Mudros and the entrance. Now in all that city of ships, so busy with passing picket-boats, and noisy with the labour of men, the getting of the anchors began. Ship after ship, crammed with soldiers, moved slowly out of harbour, in the lovely day, and felt again the heave of the sea. No such gathering of fine ships has ever been seen upon this earth, and the beauty and the exaltation of the youth upon them, made them like sacred things as they moved away. All the thousands of men aboard them, gathered on deck to see, till each rail was thronged. These men had come from all parts of the British world, from Africa, Australia, Canada, India, the Mother Country, New Zealand and remote islands in the sea. They had said good-bye to home that they might offer their lives in the cause we stand for.

In a few hours at most, as they well knew, perhaps a tenth of them would have looked their last on the sun, and be a part of foreign earth or dumb things that the tides push. Many of them would have disappeared forever from the knowledge of man, blotted from the book of life none would know how, by a fall or chance shot in the darkness, in the blast of a shell, or alone, like a hurt beast, in some scrub or gully, far from comrades and the English speech and the English singing. And perhaps a third of them would be mangled, blinded or broken, lamed, made imbecile or disfigured, with the colour and the taste of life taken from them, so that they would never more move with comrades nor exult in the sun. And those not taken thus would be under the ground, sweating in the trench, carrying sandbags up the sap, dodging death and danger, without rest or food or drink, in the blazing sun or the frost of the Gallipoli night, till death seemed relaxation and a wound a luxury. But as they moved out these things were but the end they asked, the reward they had come for, the unseen cross upon the breast. All that they felt was a gladness of exultation that their young courage was to be used. They went like kings in a pageant to the imminent death.

'His figure,
        then commanding,"

Sir Winston Churchill

The Divine Fortune, watching Life's affairs,
Justly endowed him with what Fortune may,
With sense of Storm and where the Centre lay,
With tact of deed, in some wise witty way.

Fortune of parents came in equal shares,
With England's wisest mingling with the West,
A startling newness, making better best,
A newness putting old things to a test....

So, when convulsion came, and direst need,
When, in a mess of Nations overthrown,
This England stood at bay, and stood alone,
His figure, then commanding, stood as stone,

Or, speaking, uttered like the very breed
Of Francis Drake, disaster being near,
One solemn watchword, to have done with fear.
Thence, without other drum-beat, all took cheer,
Content with such a Captain, such a Creed.

'One moonlit night...'

Sea Superstition

One moonlit night in the tropics, as my ship was slipping south under all sail, I was put to walking the deck on the lee side of the poop, with orders to watch the ship's clock and strike the bell at each half-hour. It was a duty I had done nightly for many nights, but this night was memorable to me. The sailors, as they lay sleeping in the shadows, were like august things in bronze. And the skies seemed so near me, I felt as though we were sailing through a cave, the roof of which was wrought of dim branches, as of trees, that bore the moon and the stars like shining fruits.

Gradually, however, the peace in my heart gave way to an eating melancholy, and I felt a sadness, such as has come to me but twice in my life, that was like a dark cloak over my mind. With the sadness there came a horror of the water and of the skies, till my presence in that ship, under the ghastly corpse-light of the moon, among that sea, was a terror to me past power of words to tell. I went to the ship's rail, and shut my eyes for a moment, and then opened them to look down upon the water rushing past. I had shut my eyes upon the sea, but when I opened them I looked upon the forms of the sea-spirits. The water was indeed there, hurrying aft as the ship cut through; but in the bright foam for far about the ship I saw multitudes of beautiful, inviting faces that had an eagerness and a swiftness in them unlike the speed or the intensity of human beings. I remember thinking that I had never seen anything of such passionate beauty as those faces, and as I looked at them my melancholy fell away like a rag. I felt a longing to fling myself over the rail so as to be with that inhuman beauty. Yet even as I looked that beauty became terrible, as the night had been terrible but a few seconds before. And with the changing of my emotions the faces changed. They became writhelled and hag-like: and in the leaping of the water as we rushed, I saw malevolent white hands that plucked and snapped at me. I remember I was afraid to go near the rail again before the day dawned.

'On, on! they cried, 'St George!'

Philip the King - A messenger reports

Nobly the English line
Trampled the bubbled brine;
We heard the gun-trucks whine
To the taut laniard.
Onwards we saw them forge,
While billowing at the gorge.
'On, on!' they cried, 'St George!
Down with the Spaniard!'

From their van squadron broke
A withering battle-stroke,
Tearing our plankèd oak
By straiks asunder,
Blasting the wood like rot
With such a hail of shot,
So constant and so hot
It beat us under.

The English would not close;
They fought us as they chose,
Dealing us deadly blows
For seven hours.
Lords of our chiefest rank
The bitter billow drank,
For there the English sank
Three ships of ours.

'Desolate seas we sailed, so grim...'

Philip the King - The Last of the Armada

Now our hearts failed, for food and water failed;
The men fell sick by troops, the wounded died.
They washed about the wet decks as we sailed
For want of strength to lift them overside.
Desolate seas we sailed, so grim, so wide,
That ship by ship our comrades disappeared.
With neither sun nor star to be a guide,
Like spirits of the wretched dead we steered.

Till, having beaten through the Pentland Pass,
We saw the Irish surf, with mists of spray
Blowing far inland, blasting trees and grass,
And gave God thanks, for we espied a bay
Safe, with bright water running down the clay –
A running brook where we could drink and drink.
But drawing near, our ships were cast away,
Bilged on the rocks; we saw our comrades sink....

Or worse; for those the breakers cast ashore
The Irish killed and stripped; their bodies white
Lay naked to the wolves – yea, sixty score –
All down the windy beach, a piteous sight.
The savage Irish watched by bonfire light
Lest more should come ashore; we heard them there
Screaming the bloody news of their delight,
Then we abandoned hope and new *(sic)* despair.

'A wet road heaving, shining.'

Roadways

One road leads to London,
One road leads to Wales,
My road leads me seawards
To the white dipping sails.

One road leads to the river,
As it goes singing slow;
My road leads to shipping,
Where the bronzed sailors go.

Leads me, lures me, calls me
To salt green tossing sea;
A road without earth's road-dust
Is the right road for me.

A wet road heaving, shining,
And wild with seagulls' cries,
A mad salt sea-wind blowing
The salt spray in my eyes.

My road calls me, lures me
West, east, south and north;
Most roads lead men homewards,
My road leads me forth.

To add more miles to the tally
Of grey miles left behind,
In quest of that great beauty
God put me here to find.

'Long and long ago it was...'

Posted as Missing

Under all her topsails she trembled like a stag,
The wind made a ripple in her bonny red flag;
They cheered her from the shore and they cheered her from the pier,
And under all her topsails she trembled like a deer.

So she passed swaying, where the green seas run,
Her wind-steadied topsails were stately in the sun;
There was glitter on the water from her red port-light,
So she passed swaying, till she was out of sight.

Long and long ago it was, a weary time it is,
The bones of her sailor-men are coral bones by this;
Coral plants, and shark-weed, and a mermaid's comb,
And if the fishers net them they never bring them home.

It's rough on sailors' women. They have to mangle hard,
And stitch at dungarees till their finger-ends are scarred,
Thinking of the sailor-men who sang among the crowd,
Hoisting of her topsails when she sailed so proud.

'...and it's there we went ashore,'

Spanish Waters

Spanish waters, Spanish waters, you are ringing in my ears,
Like a slow sweet piece of music from the grey forgotten years;
Telling tales, and beating tunes, and bringing weary thoughts to me
Of the sandy beach at Muertos, where I would that I could be.

There's a surf breaks on Los Muertos, and it never stops to roar,
And it's there we came to anchor, and it's there we went ashore,
Where the blue lagoon is silent amid snags of rotting trees,
Dropping like the clothes of corpses cast up by the seas.

We anchored at Los Muertos when the dipping sun was red,
We left her half-a-mile to sea, to west of Nigger Head;
And before the mist was on the Cay, before the day was done,
We were all ashore on Muertos with the gold that we had won.

We smoothed the place with mattocks, and we took and blazed the tree,
Which marks yon where the gear is hid that none will ever see,
And we laid aboard the ship again, and south away we steers,
Through the loud surf of Los Muertos which is beating in my ears.

I'm the last alive that knows it. All the rest have gone their ways
Killed, or died, or come to anchor in the old Mulatas Cays,
And I go singing, fiddling, old and starved and in despair,
And I know where all the gold is hid, if I were only there.

'...The sea roamers drive the oars...'

The Galley-Rowers

Staggering over the running combers
  The long-ship heaves her dripping flanks,
Singing together, the sea roamers
  Drive the oars grunting in the banks.
   A long pull,
   And a long long pull to Mydath

'Where are ye bound, ye swart sea-farers,
  Vexing the grey wind-angered brine,
Bearers of home-spun cloth, and bearers
  Of goat-skins filled with country wine?'

'We are bound sunset-wards, not knowing,
  Over the whale's way miles and miles,
Going to Vine-Land, haply going
  To the Bright Beach of the Blessed Isles.

'In the wind's teeth and the spray's stinging
  Westward and outward forth we go,
Knowing not whither nor why, but singing
  An old old oar-song as we row.
   A long pull,
   And a long long pull to Mydath.'

'Those bows so lovely-curving...'

Ships (A)

I cannot tell their wonder nor make known
Magic that once thrilled through me to the bone,
But all men praise some beauty, tell some tale,
Vent a high mood which makes the rest seem pale,
Pour their heart's blood to flourish one green leaf,
Follow some Helen for her gift of grief,
And fail in what they mean, whate'er they do:
You should have seen, man cannot tell to you
The beauty of the ships of that my city.

That beauty now is spoiled by the sea's pity:
For one may haunt the pier a score of times
Hearing St Nicholas' bells ring out the chimes,
Yet never see those proud ones swaying home,
With mainyards backed and bows a cream of foam,
Those bows so lovely-curving, cut so fine
Those coulters of the many-bubbled brine,
As once, long since, when all the docks were filled
With that sea beauty man has ceased to build.

Yet though their splendour may have ceased to be,
Each played her sovereign part in making me;
Now I return my thanks with heart and lips
For the great queenliness of all those ships.

'Alfred Holt's blue smokestacks...'

Ships (B)

Familiar steamers, too, majestic steamers,
Shearing Atlantic roller-tops to streamers
Umbria, Etruria, noble, still at sea,
The grandest, then, that man had brought to be.
Majestic, City of Paris, City of Rome
Forever jealous racers, out and home.
The Alfred Holt's blue smokestacks down the stream,
The fair *Arabian* with her bows a-cream.
Booth liners, Anchor liners, Red Star liners,
The marks and styles of countless ship designers.
The *Magdalena, Puno, Potosi,*
Lost *Cotopaxi,* all well known to me.

These splendid ships, each with her grace, her glory,
Her memory of old song or comrade's story,
Still in my mind the image of life's need,
Beauty in hardest action, beauty indeed.
'They built great ships and sailed them' sounds most brave,
Whatever arts we have or fail to have;
I touch my country's mind, I come to grips
With half her purpose thinking of these ships.

'In the harbour, in the island...'

Trade Winds

In the harbour, in the island, in the Spanish Seas,
Are the tiny white houses and the orange-trees,
And day-long, night-long, the cool and pleasant breeze
  Of the steady Trade Winds blowing.

There is the red wine, the nutty Spanish ale,
The shuffle of the dancers, the old salt's tale,
The squeaking fiddle, and the soughing in the sail
  Of the steady Trade Winds blowing.

And o' nights there's fire-flies and the yellow moon,
And in the ghostly palm-trees the sleepy tune
Of a quiet voice calling me, the long low croon
  Of the steady Trade Winds blowing.

'...His vast intense great world of passionate design,'

Number 543

For ages you were rock, far below light,
Crushed, without shape, earth's unregarded bone.
Then Man in all the marvel of his might
Quarried you out and burned you from the stone.

Then, being pured to essence, you were naught
But weight and hardness, body without nerve;
Then Man in all the marvel of his thought
Smithied you into form of leap and curve;

And took you, so, and bent you to his vast,
Intense great world of passionate design,
Curve after changing curve, braced and masst
To stand all tumult that can tumble brine,

And left you, this, a rampart of a ship,
Long as a street and lofty as a tower,
Ready to glide in thunder from the slip
And spear the sea with majesty of power.

I long to see you leaping to the urge
Of the great engines, rolling as you go,
Parting the seas in sunder in a surge,
Shredding a trackway like a mile of snow

With all the wester streaming from your hull
And all gear twanging shrilly as you race,
And effortless above your stern a gull
Leaning upon the blast and keeping place.

May shipwreck and collision, fog and fire,
Rock, shoal and other evils of the sea,
Be kept from you; and may the heart's desire
Of those who speed your launching come to be.

John Masefield - A Short Biography

Born in Ledbury, Herefordshire, in 1878, John Edward Masefield spent his early life in rural surroundings, his first sight of vessels afloat being the coal barges on the nearby Hereford and Gloucester Canal. His love of reading, writing and story-telling was nurtured by his mother, Caroline, who, as well as being an able inventor of stories for her children, delighted in poetry. Sadly, before Masefield was seven years old, his mother died giving birth to his sister, and he was later sent, aged ten, as a boarder to Kings School, Warwick where he began to write poetry. The school records show that he won the Lower School Prize for Divinity and English soon after arriving at the school in 1888. He left the school (ran away) after a particularly gruelling Latin test, set for all boys below the 6th Form, in the summer of 1891, his mark being 10%. This is hardly surprising as today that same test would be considered difficult for A-level pupils. Not long after, his father, George, died following a mental breakdown and Masefield was taken under the guardianship of an uncle and aunt, the latter strongly disapproving of his bookish nature. Many years later, in the Michaelmas term of 1928, Masefield was the guest of honour at the school's annual prize-giving. All went well other than for many having to be turned away – Masefield attracted a full house. He is reputed to have said, 'I hope all you boys are happy here. I wasn't - I ran away!' Masefield's grand-daughter contends it is not strictly true to say he ran away because, instead of taking to the road, he stole a punt and went down the Avon.

John Masefield on board HMS Conway *with officers and cadets 1930*

Desiring more manly endeavours of him, Masefield's guardians enrolled him, in 1891, as a cadet in the training ship HMS *Conway,* then moored in the River Mersey. There, in addition to the nautical training he received, he was introduced to the maritime history, mythology and yarns that were to become the essence of much of his later works. Leaving *Conway* in 1894, he shipped aboard the four-masted barque, *Gilcruix,* sailing from Cardiff to Iquique, Chile, around Cape Horn. After some while there, he became so ill that, following a period in hospital, he was classed as DBS (a Distressed British Seaman) and shipped by steamer back to England. His aunt, as ever unsympathetic to his experience, condition and reaction to life at sea, sent Masefield to join another ship in New York.

Masefield says, 'I deserted my ship in New York and cut myself adrift from her, and from my home. I was going to be a writer, come what may.' Drifting around for a while, he eventually found a job in a carpet factory where the money and regular hours gave him the means and the time to buy and read the not inconsiderable library he built up. After two years, he shipped on a steamer from New York and worked his passage back to England as a steerage steward. Here, his writing output, in the form of poetry, children's books, naval histories, novels and literary criticism was as great as time and his health allowed. His work as a bank clerk and recurring bouts of ill health, mainly malaria, left scant opportunity to construct and pursue, to its full extent, the literary career he had set his sights on.

It was in 1902 that Masefield met Caroline Crommelin, eleven years his senior, a scholar in Classics and English Literature and a teacher of Mathematics. She took a great interest in his work and he found her encouragement to be an enabling factor. They married in 1903 and had two children, Judith (in 1904) and Lewis (in 1910.) In the same year, aged 24, Masefield published his first collection of works under the title *Salt-Water Ballads,* included in which was one of his best known poems, *Sea Fever:*

> *I must go down to the sea again, to the lonely sea and the sky,*
> *And all I ask is a tall ship and a star to steer her by.*

Also included in that collection was his poem, *A Consecration,* an early statement of intent to tell it how it was:

Not the ruler for me, but the ranker, the
tramp of the road,
The slave with the sack on his shoulders
pricked on with the goad,
The man with too weighty a burden, too
weary a load.
The sailor, the stoker of steamers, the
man with the clout,
The chantyman bent at the halliards
putting a tune to the shout,
The drowsy man at the wheel and the
tired look-out.
Of these shall my songs be fashioned, my
tales be told."

Not for him the romantic view spoken of by his contemporary, Rudyard Kipling who wrote of "Great steamers white and gold." Masefield nailed his colours to the mast with the above words, and elsewhere said, 'It will be a good thing for England when painters and poets leave off painting and ranting about fishing smacks and pirates and "the deep blue sea" and take to showing, with their best ability, the real life of the poor fellows who bring them not only their luxuries but their very food.'

Masefield worked steadily for a while without any great success, although his output did enable him to take up writing full time. He worked at one stage on the *Manchester Guardian* and, of his pieces published in *The Tatler* and *Pall Mall Magazine,* he said, 'My ballads are being taken as fast as I can write them.' 1911 saw the publication of his long narrative poem, *The Everlasting Mercy,*

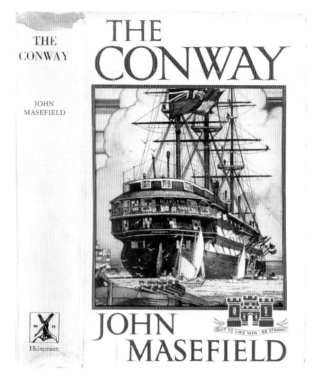

described by J M Barrie as 'incomparably the finest literature'. Two further poems, again of the long, narrative genre, *The Widow in the Bye Street* and *Dauber*, were published in 1912 and 1914 respectively.

When the Great War broke out in 1914, Masefield was over the age of military service. Nevertheless, he played his part, firstly with service as an orderly at a British Red Cross hospital in France and later in charge of hospital motor boats in the Dardenelles. His experiences in these two theatres of war led to two lecture tours of the United States of America where he highlighted the 'positives' that the Allies had

gained from the Dardanelles campaign and encouraged US citizens to enlist and join the fight against the Imperial German Army. On the second of these two tours, the universities of Harvard and Yale both awarded him Honorary Doctorates of Letters. Masefield recorded the Dardanelles campaign in his book *Gallipoli,* which was an instant success, described by one critic as 'too sacred for applause'. He was invited by Sir Douglas Haig to write similarly on the battle of the Somme but, denied access to official documents, he was unable to replicate that literary success. He did, however, produce two short volumes, covering events to the best of his ability with the material available to him, *The Old Front Line* and *The Battle of the Somme.*

After the war, Masefield returned to the long narrative style of poetry with the publication of *Reynard the Fox, Right Royal* and *King Cole.* They told, in that order, the story of a fox hunt, a steeple-chase and of a travelling circus. Perhaps remembering how well the USA had received the presentation of his lectures, Masefield began to promote poetry as a performing art rather than merely that to be written and read. He established the Oxford Recitations, a verse-speaking competition held in Oxford, and helped to establish the Oxford Summer Diversions – a festival of recitals, plays and ballet.

In 1930, on the death of the Poet Laureate, Robert Bridges, and on the recommendation of the Prime Minister, Ramsay MacDonald,

Masefield was appointed to the vacant post by King George V. This was a popular choice and ahead of notable contemporaries including Kipling, Dryden, Houseman, de la Mare and Yeats. In the same year, he received the freedom of the City of Hereford and was elected to Honorary Membership of the Honourable Company of Master Mariners. He had, in 1922, been awarded an Honorary Doctorate from Oxford University and the same honour was conferred by Cambridge University in 1931. Other honorary degrees came from the University of Wales and from the universities of Liverpool, St Andrews, Sheffield and London.

However, perhaps the crowning glory to Masefield's literary career was his being awarded the Order of Merit, announced in the Birthday Honours List, 3rd June 1935. He took his Poet Laureate duties seriously, celebrating many notable events in the life of the British people with short but apposite verse. Further awards followed in later years including those from the Royal Society of Literature (Companion of Literature), the William Foyle Poetry Prize and from the

National Book League. He became President of the Society of Authors in 1937, a position formerly held by Tennyson, Hardy and Barrie.

A serious illness in 1949 meant that little further work of note was produced, the exceptions being *So Long to Learn: Chapters of an Autobiography* in 1952 and later, an LP and three further discs,

recording some of his works as the spoken word. His wife, Constance, died in 1960. Sadly their son, Lewis, predeceased his mother, having been killed by artillery fire while serving with the RAMC in North Africa during World War II. Masefield died on 12th May 1967 and his ashes were interred in Poets' Corner, Westminster Abbey.

When I am buried, all my thoughts and acts
Will be reduced to lists of dates and facts.

John Edward Masefield OM

Poet Laureate

1878 - 1967

Footnote.

The following short extract is taken from a paper titled, *The Idea of a Maritime Museum,* presented by Dr C Northcote Parkinson, and first published in Transactions Vol. 3 of the Liverpool Nautical Research Society for 1947. It opens with the words, 'In attempting to interest you in the idea of a Maritime Museum in Liverpool....' After propounding his idea at length, the writer closes with the words, 'And somewhere near the entrance, I can imagine a statue of John Masefield, the poet of Merseyside and perhaps our greatest poet of the sea.'

Now, there's a thought.

Kenneth D Shoesmith - A Short Biography

Kenneth Denton Shoesmith was born on 11th June 1890 at No 7 Heathfield Terrace, Skircoat, Halifax, West Yorkshire, his mother being Mary Hannah, daughter of Denton Shoesmith, market gardener of that address. As there is no father's name entered upon the birth certificate, it would perhaps be politically correct to say that Kenneth was born into a one-parent family. Shortly after, the young Kenneth, with mother and grandmother, moved to No 9 Imperial Terrace, Claremont Park, Blackpool, where, according to the 1901 Census, the occupants are grandmother Jane (occupation - Lettings) mother Mary H (single), grandson Kenneth D, a servant and two 'visitors living on own means'. The young Shoesmith was drawing from the time he could hold a pencil and examples of his very earliest works, drawn on any available scrap of paper, including the Blackpool lodging house letterheads, survive. These are held, with a most substantial collection of his later works, by The Ulster Museum, Belfast, while many other examples are held in private collections around the world.

Shoesmith's junior talent was nurtured initially by his being enlisted into The Revival of Youthful Art League, a correspondence course, under the tutelage of Mr T R Ablett of the Royal Drawing Society, whose constructive criticism and encouragement doubtless played a part in his protégé's winning of several prizes, the earliest being The President's Prize, Gold Star in 1903. At that time, the President was the Duchess of Argyll, Princess Louise, 6th child of Queen Victoria and Prince Albert, who later

bought one of Shoesmith's watercolours. Up to the age of 17, Shoesmith continued to submit his work for appraisal, this being carefully filed away in albums with his mentor's comments and suggestions that were later to be put to such good effect. 'Finally,' Shoesmith records, 'I was sent to that university of so many fine sailors, the training ship *Conway*.' This was in 1906 when HMS *Conway* was moored in the River Mersey and where, ten years earlier, John Masefield had also been a cadet.

Upon finishing his cadetship in *Conway*, Shoesmith signed indentures with Royal Mail Steam Packet Company on 4th August 1908 and by experience, examination and hard-earned promotion, rose to the position of Chief Officer. Upon cessation of hostilities in 1918, he left the sea to take up painting full time. Eighteen years later, Shoesmith is quoted as saying, 'I have been fond of drawing since I was old enough to hold a pencil; in fact it was my craze for drawing ships that made me adopt the sea as a career. In those days (in *Conway*), the Mersey afforded an endless pageant of lovely ships, and most of my leisure on the *Conway* was spent in watching them and trying to get them down in my sketch book.' Reflecting on his time at sea, he said, 'In the harbours of the Far East and at sea in the North and South Atlantic, I was constantly excited by the sight of strange craft. More often than not, my "watch below" was spent with pencil and sketchbook in some snug corner of the deck.' He went on, 'When I was appointed Chief Officer, I had to put a curb on my hobby. The Chief of a modern liner is never really off-duty and I had no time to follow my artistic inclinations. I held on until the war ended and then - well, I wanted to paint and the sea would not spare me the time - so I gave up the sea.'

On 18th April 1916, Shoesmith married Sarah (Sadie) Ritchie, daughter of a wealthy Belfast shipowner. They had met when she was enjoying a voyage on one of the Royal Mail Steam Packet vessels, probably *Magdalena (overleaf)*. For many years, the Shoesmiths lived in Alyth Gardens, Golders Green, moving in 1935 to Willifield Way, Hampstead Garden Suburb. The estate agent's prospectus for the property at that time described it as 'a well built and very attractive bungalow residence with handsome and lofty studio 18ft x 23ft with north

top and east windows.' His output from that studio was prodigious, with much of it being commissioned by the Publicity Department of Royal Mail Lines and other leading British steamship companies. If I had to choose the two foremost examples of his work that survive today, they would be *The Defeat of the Spanish Armada* and the murals on board RMS *Queen Mary*.

The former consists of twelve panels in oils painted in 1930 to grace the drawing room of Lord Vesty, (owner of Blue Star Line) at his home, Kingswood, Dulwich. They depict the story from the Armada being sighted coming up the Channel through to the triumphant return of the English fleet to Dover. The Vesty family donated the set to Radley College Oxford in

1945 and they were subsequently sold at auction in 1998. Since then, they have appeared in various lots at auction, the latest being in Edinburgh in 2016 where one panel alone, showing Drake playing bowls on Plymouth Hoe, carried a catalogue estimate of £5,000 to £7,000.

In 1934, when the Cunard Steamship Company placed an order with John Brown Shipbuilders for the construction of Yard No 534, many of the finest artists and designers were commissioned to submit their work for consideration as being fit to grace the interior of what was to be the pride of the Cunard fleet. Since her maiden voyage in 1936 and through service during World War II across the oceans of the world as a troopship, *Queen Mary,* as she was named upon launching, has survived to this day and is afloat as a hotel, events and conference centre at Long Beach, California. Shoesmith's work was among those accepted and the magnificent murals he produced in his studio *(right)* are still on public display on board.

The *Hampstead & Highgate Express* carried an obituary for Shoesmith on 14th April 1939, from which the following is extracted:

> As a poster artist, which Shoesmith always described himself as being, he was quite definitely in the front rank of those who are content to paint what they see and know. He was direct in his methods, sound in his drawing and brilliant in his colour. His ships were not only correct in

> detail but they were always in and not on the water, for he painted with a seaman's knowledge as well as an artist's perception. He was uninfluenced by any of the schools of art, he was concerned only with what he knew and to tell the whole truth about that. He struck no attitudes, adopted no poses; his watchword was sincerity, his aim the truth. As soon as he gave up the sea and took to painting it, he achieved success, for he knew what he was doing. It was not the result of study but of experience. There are artists who have studied the sea in her moodiness; Shoesmith knew all these moods and could put them swiftly and precisely onto canvas. He had a very accurate sense of values and a gorgeous sense of humour, masculine in its vigour but never flamboyant in its expression.

He was never disturbed by criticism. There are some artists who put all of themselves into their work and leave nothing for the everyday-ness of life. Shoesmith was too much of a man to do that. He put all of his artistry into his pictures, and had still enough of himself left to make his friendship a prize.

The following obituary appeared in the *Seven Seas Club Magazine* in March 1939:

As we go to press we have received the terribly sad news of the death of Kenneth D Shoesmith RI. It is a great shock to all old members of the Club to whom 'K.D.' was so well known. After he left the Conway in '07 he went to the R.S.M.P. and left them shortly after the War to pursue his natural bent as an Artist. Being a sailorman, his marine pictures were always true and, although much of his work was used in the commercial world, his art was never 'commercialised'. He has several fine paintings in the Queen Mary, *notably the screen over the fireplace in the first class smoke room. His name will always be with the Seven Seas Club as his picture, 'Old Ships and Shipmates' has been the cover picture of our magazine for many years. One of the most genial and happiest souls it has been our fortune to meet, it seems so hard that he should pass on at the comparatively early age of 48. His name will be perpetuated for all time*

within his old ship Conway, for he painted the truly wonderful War Memorial Screen which has been the admiration of everyone who has been privileged to visit the lower deck of that famous ship.

To Mrs Shoesmith we convey our deepest sympathy in her irreparable loss and, whenever the 'old hands' of the Club are gathered together, the name of Kenneth Shoesmith cannot fail to be remembered but with the deepest affection.

Following his cremation at Golders Green Cemetery, Shoesmith's ashes were scattered from the Royal Mail Line's *Asturias (above)* in the English Channel, a fitting end for a man who not only loved the sea and the ships thereon, but had the ability to transform that love into the pictures we are still able to enjoy today.

Even as he spoke his busy pencil moved,
Drawing the leap of water off the side.
Where the great clipper trampled iron-hooved,
Making the blue hills of the sea divide.

From Dauber *by John Masefield*

Kenneth Denton Shoesmith

Member of the Royal Institute of Painters in Water Colours

1890 - 1939

Notes

On reading these notes, it will become apparent they are heavily biased towards Shoesmith's illustrations, these being within the editor's sphere of knowledge. Scholarly comment on Masefield's poems and prose falls outside that sphere but is well served by the works of Philip W Errington, a leading Masefield authority, as listed in the Bibliography. The notes that follow draw, in many instances, upon his writing.

In selecting a Shoesmith painting to accompany a particular piece of Masefield's work, it has not always been possible to obtain an exact match. While we have examples of the few specially commissioned Shoesmith paintings for Masefield's book covers, the latter's works were otherwise without illustration. At first glance, much of Masefield's work appears to speak of the romance of the sea or rather, caters for the romantic notion landlubbers may have of it. This approach, however, does not hide his underlying determination to deal with the everyday hardships faced by seafarers, and their pragmatic approach to them.

Masefield's reference to painters at sea, as in *Dauber,* may allude to his own modest pretentions as a marine artist or perhaps to the fact that most ships carried, and perhaps still carry, at least one member of the crew who is an aspiring painter. In earlier years, midshipmen were either encouraged or compelled to keep their own log of each voyage, with illustrations forming an important part. I have in my possession Shoesmith's log of his voyage to the Far East in 1909 aboard Royal Mail Steam Packet Co's (RMSPCo) *Monmouthshire*. He was serving at that time as an indentured, uncertificated deck officer, by any other name a midshipman, and an extract from his log is shown below. Before the advent of photography, the illustrations within could be as much an aid to navigation as a chart, certainly for coastal passages, landfalls and harbour approaches.

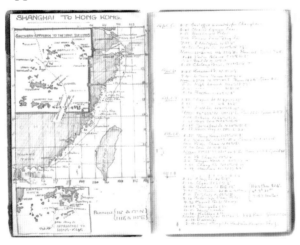

P15. A Steerage Steward

First published and sole appearance in the *Manchester Guardian*, June 1906.

This is perhaps not the actual liner on which Masefield took passage but typical of the day. Shoesmith was a member of the British Society of Poster Designers and modestly described himself as a poster artist. He was obviously more than that, but this poster depicting one of Cunard Line's four stackers at New York is an excellent example of his ability to capture the majesty of the ship in the style of the day. Posters were designed to sell passage tickets and, in this respect, I am sure Cunard would have been pleased with the result.

P17. Sea Fever

First published in *Salt-Water Ballads* London, Grant Richards, November 1902. A collection of poems which had, by then, appeared in newspapers and periodicals.

In several printed editions, the word *go* is omitted, as in 'I must down to the sea'. I have shown the version with *go* included, as it appears in my father's 1931 edition of *The Collected Poems of John Masefield*. London, William Heinemann. Note that *go* is omitted from verses two and three in this edition. Masefield later admitted to the variations but always included *go* in his recitation of the poem. This evocative painting of a ship under full sail beneath a starry sky appears in various publications and features on the front of Philip W Errington's book, *Sea-Fever*.

P19. The Bird of Dawning

First published London, William Heinemann, November 1933.

This classic sea adventure tells of the *Blackgauntlet* and her homeward-bound race from China to London. Disaster strikes when, at night, the ship is in collision with a steamer. Half the ship's crew manage to escape in the lifeboat while the other half perish, leaving

Cruiser, the young Second Mate, to take command. This watercolour study is an example of Shoesmith's junior work showing his progress in mastering the portrayal of a ship under full sail, his inspiration coming from the painting, *Off Valparaiso* by Thomas Somerscales. Shoesmith went on to feature the ship in many of his later paintings and posters.

P21. Dauber (A)

First published William Heinemann London 1913.

A long, narrative poem in seven parts with a total of two hundred and sixty-one verses, each of seven lines. On joining the ship, it soon becomes apparent the Dauber is neither a good seaman nor painter and consequently suffers the contempt of his shipmates. A gradual improvement during the voyage brings Dauber to a point where he begins to earn the respect of the crew. Sadly, before he can enjoy that status, he dies in a fall from the rigging. Just as Masefield would have written ideas down as they came to him for future use in his poems and prose, so Shoesmith sketched both for reference and recreation. Some sketches were for presentation to a shipping company's publicity department for acceptance before work commenced on the finished article, while others were of a quality sufficient for them to be used in their own right. This particular drawing is a case in point and was used by the Seven Seas Club for the front of their magazine in 1926.

P23. Dauber (B)

This wave study is an exercise carried out by Shoesmith as part of the art correspondence course he undertook before joining *Conway*, so before 1906. It was kept by his proud mother, along with many other examples of his work under the tutelage of T R Ablett of the Royal Drawing Society and now forms part of the Ulster Museum's Shoesmith collection in Belfast.

P25. The *Conway* Part I

The *Conway*'s words to the new-comer. From Masefield's book, *The Conway*, first published London 1933 by William Heinemann and dedicated to Captain and Mrs Broadbent.

Captain Broadbent was at one time Captain Superintendent in *Conway* and in retirement, founded the Seven Seas Club of which Masefield became a member. I count this painting, *Conway and Mauretania in the River Mersey*, as the crowning glory of all Shoesmith's works; it was certainly the painting that ignited my interest in this artist, and the inspiration for me to write the book, *The Maritime Art of Kenneth D Shoesmith*. Sadly, after a brief exhibition at the Ulster Museum, Belfast, in 2013, the picture was returned to the Museum's archive storage, where it remains today, unseen by the general public. In *The Conway*, Masefield wrote, '1917. One foggy morning the *Mauretania* came so close that Tommy Wetham and Bill Finch, another instructor, are supposed to have pushed her off from the chains with a couple of boat-hooks.' Masefield wrote of another *Conway* instructor, Wallace Blair, in his poem *One of Wally's Yarns*, describing him as 'a most gifted storyteller, a yarn-spinner of the old dogwatch kind'.

P27. Cargoes

First published in *A Broad Sheet* in 1903 and later, in the same year in *Ballads,* a book of Masefield's collected poems, London, Elkin Mathews.

John Betjeman suggested that this poem, along with *Sea Fever,* would remain "as long as the language lasts". Once again I have failed in my endeavours to match Masefield's words with a Shoesmith painting, this time that of a quinquireme. Stately Spanish galleons feature elsewhere in the book, so this poem provided an opportunity to feature one of Shoesmith's paintings that echoes the sentiment of Masefield's opening words to the third verse of *Cargoes*. While the words, 'Dirty British coaster', might in this instance be substituted by 'Rusty British tramp ship', the Red Ensign, visible at the stern, would have been a feature common to both. The Nore, a sandbank at the mouth of the Thames Estuary and a hazard to shipping, received the world's first lightship in 1732. This has since been replaced by Sea Reach No 1 Buoy. Another painting that would serve just as well to illustrate Masefield's list of cargoes carried by a dirty British coaster is this one, titled *Leaving the Coal Tips (overleaf)*.

P29. Port Of Many Ships

First published in *The Speaker*, August 1902.

One of four Shoesmith originals in my possession, this watercolour would have been painted on a speculative basis and offered to the publicity department of a shipping company for consideration, acceptance and use as they might see fit. While I have not seen this particular one used in that commercial capacity, others (see *Spanish Waters*) of a similar style and subject were.

P31. For all Seafarers

Published in *Merchantmen at War*, London, His Majesty's Stationery Office 1944.

During World Wars I and II, many merchant ships were taken up from trade by the Admiralty to serve a variety of purposes, this particular liner of the RMSPCo being a typical example. Given a coat of grey paint and lightly armed, her role was to cruise the North Sea as part of the 10th Cruiser Squadron's blockade of north German ports at the beginning of World War I. Particularly unsuited to this work, these armed merchant cruisers (AMCs) became known as Admiralty Made Coffins; their lack of armour plating being no match for the heavy guns aboard ships of the Imperial German Navy.

P33. The Wanderer

From Masefield's book *The Wanderer of Liverpool,* published London, William Heinemann in October 1930, re-printed in the same month and again in November of the same year.

It was dedicated to All Old Wanderers. The ship was designed and built by Mr W H Potter at Queen's Dock, Liverpool as Yard No 150. She was 309' long by 46' wide and with a depth of 25.8', having a carrying capacity of 4,500 tons. Masefield said of the ship, 'She had a noble sheer, a beautiful bow and an exquisite elliptical stern.' At the invitation of the RMSPCo and other large British shipping companies in the 1920s and 1930s, Mr and Mrs Shoesmith were able to enjoy one or two cruises each year at the company's expense. As the saying goes, 'There is no such thing as a free lunch' and these cruises were no exception. Cruising the Baltic Sea and Norwegian fjords in the summer months and the Mediterranean later in the season, Shoesmith was required to produce around sixteen paintings that would be put to use in the company's advertising programme, many of them appearing in calendar form. With a free rein to paint what he saw during these cruises, Shoesmith took full advantage to capture the beauty of craft that crossed his bow; this particular ship under full sail and the vessel illustrating *Sea Superstition* being good examples. Evidence in pictorial form also exists of the Shoesmiths' cruises to South America, the West Indies and, courtesy of Canadian Pacific Railways, a trip across the Rocky Mountains, as shown here.

P35. The Ambulance Ship

From *Soho Centenary*, London, Hutchinson & Co Ltd. 1944.

Another example of ships taken up from trade by the British Government in World War I, this RMSPCo liner, *Essequibo,* has been converted to a hospital ship. Conspicuous markings and the international conventions of the day initially gave such ships immunity from enemy attack. As the war progressed, however, they came to be considered by the Imperial German Navy as legitimate targets. As such, they were attacked and sunk with the tragic loss of life not only of wounded soldiers but also of nursing staff and doctors, many of them being volunteers. Shoesmith was a serving officer of the British mercantile marine with RMSPCo throughout the war, and this particular painting would undoubtedly have been made at that time from personal observation.

P37. The Tarry Buccaneer

Published in *Salt-Water Ballads*, London, Grant Richards 1902 and dedicated to Jack B Yeats.

Set to the tune, *The Fine Old English Gentleman*, written in 1835 by Henry Russell, a composer, pianist, singer and lyricist. Another original Shoesmith in my possession, this painting is not of the Spanish Main of which Masefield writes in this poem, but of the North African coast. Research shows the figurehead to be that of Barbarossa, the most feared of the Barbary pirates who plundered rich pickings from the many ships passing through the Straits of Gibraltar carrying freight between Britain and the Mediterranean ports.

P39. The Conway - Rowing

From Masefield's book, *The Conway.*

I have yet to meet a former Conway who does not have fond memories of his cadet days nor speak of the experience as other than having made him fit for whatever his adult life might have thrown at him; an epitome of the ship's motto, *Quit ye like men, be strong.*

Shoesmith was no exception and was most generous in the donation of many of his works to his alma mater. These were put to use as covers for the ship's prospectus, showing the parents of prospective cadets the experience their sons might enjoy for the fees they would pay. As Masefield says, 'Rowing was a daily or almost daily duty....' It would have had the double benefit of instilling the cadets with the discipline of working as a team while also providing healthy exercise. An unfortunate side-effect of the latter would be the production of an appetite that ship-board fare might occasionally fail to satisfy. The Sloyne is a deep water anchorage in the River Mersey which, many years after *Conway* moved to the Menai Strait, was the location of the Tranmere Oil Terminal. This photograph *(right)* by Mr William Cull of Prenton, Birkenhead, is titled *Gig's Crews* and features in Masefield's book.

P41. Victorious Troy or The *Hurrying Angel*

The first English edition of this book by Masefield was published London, William Heinemann October, 1935.

The novel concerns a ship, the *Hurrying Angel,* hit by a cyclone in the South Pacific, and tells of the unlikely saviour of the vessel. Shoesmith's illustration used for the dust jacket of the book shows the state of the *Hurrying Angel* after the 'lumping, following sea' had wreaked its havoc. It depicts the vessel with 'a jagged, cracked, hollow, sharp tooth of yellow iron some thirty foot high; it was the stump of the mainmast.' Unfortunately, the dust jacket of my copy of this book also looks as if it has been through a similar experience and, with a crease down the middle, is in no fit state to be reproduced here. Instead, another painting by Shoesmith which fits Masefield's description of the situation immediately before the fateful following seas struck. To match the text, the ship is shown 'putting her snout down into it'. The dust jacket bears one of the few pictures expressly painted by Shoesmith for Masefield's work and gives a tantalising glimpse of what a full collaboration might have produced. This is my book's *raison d'etre*.

P43. After forty years

These verses open Part II of *The Conway*.

Masefield writes of an evening in *Conway* on the River Mersey when, indeed, he would have seen 'the lights of steamers passing to the sea'. Also visible would have been the lights ashore at Rock Ferry, Birkenhead and at the Pier Head, Liverpool. Shoesmith's painting is one used for the cover of a Dinner Adieu menu for cruise ships of the RMSPCo during the 1920s and 1930s. Many of these would have been signed by one's fellow passengers and kept as a souvenir. This particular example was found in an old album of black and white photographs recording one passenger's Norwegian fjord cruise aboard *Asturias*.

P45. Captain Stratton's Fancy

From *The Speaker*, 9th May 1903.

The feeling of comradeship Shoesmith had for his fellow cadets spilled over to those of the Seven Seas Club of which both he and Masefield were members. The club was founded in 1922 by *Conway*'s Captain Superintendent, Captain W H Broadbent. Generous again in donating the fruits of his artistic skill, this time to the Seven Seas Club, Shoesmith's drawing, *Old Ships and Shipmates*, often adorns the front of the Club's monthly dinner menu. While the rig of the day for these meetings is now normally lounge suit, and liquid refreshment taken in glasses rather than tankards, the spirit of the meetings has been well captured. *Don't Forget Your Old Shipmates* is a traditional song from the days of Nelson's Navy.

> *We're the boys who fear no noise*
> *Whilst the thundering cannons roar,*
> *And long we've toiled on the rolling wave,*
> *And now we're safe on shore.*

At the Seven Seas Club's Trafalgar Night Dinner, a tot of old Navy rum is drunk to toast *The Immortal Memory*. The Royal Navy rum ration or tot, the daily amount of rum issued to sailors on Royal Navy ships, was abolished in 1970.

P47. 1959 – HMS Conway's Centenary Year.

From *HMS Conway 1859–1974*, written by Alfie Windsor (Conway Cadet 1964–68) and published Livingstone EH5, Witherby Seamanship International 2008.

A service of commemoration and thanksgiving was held at Bangor Cathedral on 28th July 1959, followed by the Centenary Prize Day and parade at Plas Newydd*. The guest of honour was Lord Cilcennin, previous First Lord of the Admiralty. Masefield wrote this as a special verse for the occasion. Another of Shoesmith's contributions to his old ship. Royal Navy ships in the background will be those built or under repair at Cammell, Laird & Co, Shipbuilders and Repairers, Birkenhead.

*The land base of HMS *Conway* on Anglesey following the loss of the old ship in 1953.

P49. St Mary's Bells

Ballads, London, Elkin Mathews 1903.

In this poem, Masefield airs the traditional view most seafarers had of a better life to come, and follows the theme he expresses in *Port Of Many Ships*, 'It's a sunny pleasant anchorage...' While a pessimistic sailor might speak of Davy Jones's Locker, with the finality that place-name conveys, his optimistic 'oppo' would prefer to think of his final resting place in the terms of that expressed by Masefield. These echo the hope expressed in the words of the traditional seafarer's song *Fiddler's Green*.

> *Now Fiddler's Green is a place I've heard tell*
> *Where the fishermen go if they don't go to Hell,*
> *Where the skies are all clear and the dolphins do play,*
> *And the cold coast of Greenland is far, far away.*
>
> *Where the skies are all clear and there's never a gale*
> *And the fish jump on board with one swish of their tail.*
> *Where you lie at your leisure, there's no work to do,*
> *And the skipper's below making tea for the crew.*

Wrap me up in my tarpaulin jacket,
No more on the docks I'll be seen.
Just tell my old shipmates
I'm taking a trip, mates,
And I'll see you one day on Fiddler's
Green.

Once again, and perhaps unsurprisingly, unable to find an exactly matching Shoesmith painting for *Holy Mary by San Marie Lagoon*, I have used editor's licence and opted for this tranquil scene of fishermen seemingly at leisure on their boats. The scale of the painting, on the doors of an altar screen, can be seen from the black and white photo *(right)* showing their installation on board *Queen Mary*. I thought the picture appropriate when you see what the doors hid from view other than on Sundays.

Unfortunately, the doors are no longer on display as an installation, but I have been assured they are still in safe storage on board. But how safe is safe with doubt having been cast over the ship's long-term future?

P51. For the Men of the Merchant Navy and Fishing Fleets

From *Merchant Navy Week*, Portsmouth, Gale & Polden 1937.

As mentioned previously, most of Shoesmith's commercial output appeared on posters, postcards, calendars and ship-board literature such as menus and passenger lists. This painting made it to the thinner ranks of the book jacket, in particular, that of *The ABC of Fish*

Cooking, an exhortation (propaganda thinly disguised as a cookery book) to British housewives in the 1920s and 1930s to buy fish in support of the nation's fishing industry. 'There's all the health of the sea in fish,' reads the introduction and, we are told, 'A fish diet suits everyone, provides nourishment for the worker, energy for growing children, easily digested food for the invalid and dainty dishes for "fussy" appetites. All as simple as ABC.' Not bad for sixpence!

P53. A Valediction

The Collected Poems of John Masefield, first published 1923.

The distinctive design of this ship's stern readily identifies her as the ship shown earlier (see *The*

Wanderer). Here we see her at night in calmer waters with hardly a cat's paw to ruffle the water or fill her sails. The picture, for a RMSPCo calendar, is one I would describe as being of the Shoesmith intermediate stage. The first stage saw his depiction of the Company's ship as the main subject, filling the frame so to speak. This painting shows the liner as a secondary subject, albeit the sailing ship's angle into the picture leads the viewer's eye to the desired object. An example of what I think of as his final stage can be seen in *Trade Winds* – not a ship in sight! Masefield gives the fourth line of each verse the echo of a shanty.

P55. The Seven Seas Shanty Book containing 42 Sea Shanties and Songs

London, Boosey & Co Ltd., 1927.

As a member of the Seven Seas Club and one of its literary luminaries, it was perhaps natural that John Masefield should have been asked to provide a foreword to the Club's book of collected songs of this genre. Appropriate too that we should use the book's cover illustration to accompany his words. On the same theme is this pen and ink drawing titled *The Monkey's Orphan, (below),* the nickname given to a ship's fiddler. By 1926, it had become a custom at the Seven Seas Club in London to hold a shanty sing-along after the Club's monthly dinners. When writing elsewhere of shanties, Masefield gives preference to the alternative spelling, *chanties.*

P57. Gallipoli

Published London, William Heinemann 1916.

Masefield recorded the realities of Gallipoli in his eponymous book from first-hand experience. He had been in charge of motor launches taking wounded troops from the beaches to waiting hospital ships anchored in deeper water some way off shore. Shoesmith records in this contemporary painting the final

evacuation of troops (December 1915 to January 1916) to the RMSPCo's *Cardiganshire,* taken up from trade by the British Government to serve as a troopship. At that time, Shoesmith was serving in RMSPCo's *Magdalena,* which may have been active there in the same capacity. Shoesmith was *Cardiganshire*'s acting Second Officer from November 1913 to July 1914 and her Chief Officer in late 1917. For one who began his maritime career in HMS *Conway,* Shoesmith's final posting before retiring from the sea was as Chief Officer in RMSPCo's *Conway;* rather apt, I thought. Here she is *(right)* in her wartime Dazzle-Paint.

P59. Sir Winston Churchill

The Times, 25th January 1965.

A speedy response from the Poet Laureate as Churchill had died only the day before. The Dardanelles campaign had failed to complete its objective, set by Winston Churchill, (then First Lord of the Admiralty and thus political head of the Royal Navy), to secure British maritime access to the Black Sea ports of Russia. Held accountable (blamed) for this failure by many (other than the likes of Masefield, whose book contrived an heroic spin) Churchill's success as a war leader in World War II came as a revelation to his earlier detractors. Masefield's loyalty to Churchill appears to have held firm as evidenced by this short poem. The black and white photo shows Churchill at a press conference in the Tourist Class Drawing Room on board *Queen Mary* on one of his several

dashes across the North Atlantic for talks with the US President and his senior senators. The mural on the wall behind Churchill is one by Shoesmith that survives *in situ* today. The room is now a gift shop and, from personal observation, I know the mural is overlooked by visitors or not recognised and appreciated for the work of art it most definitely is.

P61. Sea Superstition

First published in the *Manchester Guardian,* 5th December 1903.

Certainly this painting shows the 'moonlit night' of which Masefield wrote, but the type of craft, an Arab dhow, is more likely sailing not 'in the tropics' but in the eastern Mediterranean or Arabian Sea. Again, this is one of what I term Shoesmith's intermediate paintings, almost certainly for a calendar, where the subject ship leads one's eye to the object in the distance, a cruise liner of the RMSPCo. The original painting was kindly loaned to me for a while by its owner, the renowned automobile artist,

Barry Rowe, whose beautifully evocative paintings of vintage racing cars of the 1920s–30s chime with Shoesmith's posters of that era.

P63. Philip the King – a messenger reports

Philip the King and Other Poems, London, William Heinemann 1914.

Written by Masefield in the form of a play, this epic records, from start to finish, the events known in English history as The Spanish Armada, from the Spanish king's perspective. The painting is one of twelve murals commissioned by the 1st Lord Vesty (owner of the Blue Star Line) to decorate the walls of his dining room. Each panel is 40" deep with widths varying to suit the dimensions of the room. At the end of World War II, they were donated by the Vesty family to Radley College, Oxford in memory of Lord Vesty's son, a former pupil, Captain William Vesty, Scots Guards, killed in action in 1944. Sold by the college at auction in 1998, the murals have since appeared at various other auctions, where successive hammer prices have slipped below those previously achieved. This would be due, no doubt, to changing tastes and possibly the sheer size of each panel. I have in the past endeavoured to establish the identity of each new owner without success, the auction houses' confidentiality requirements making mine a lost cause. My feeling, however, is that the successful bidders are unlikely to be Spanish nationals.

P65. Philip the King – The Last of the Armada

Depicting the final fate of the Spanish fleet, we see here the vessels being wrecked on the south coast of Ireland, battered by the Atlantic gale that drove them ashore to death and destruction when, in Masefield's words, 'we abandoned hope and knew despair'.

P67. Roadways

The Speaker 2nd May 1903.

It might seem strange that Masefield, whose first voyage under sail ended in his return home by steamer as a DBS and whose second ended in his jumping ship, should later write, '...my road...leads me, lures me, calls me to salt green tossing sea'. His very description of the sea might be enough to deter those readers with a weak stomach from taking the coast road, let alone 'a wet road, heaving, shining'. There were, however, and still are, plenty of armchair seafarers who buy into his vision. This Shoesmith illustration is from a book *The Wonderful Story of the Sea* in a chapter entitled *Perils of the Ocean Highway*. The caption to the painting reads 'Dirty Weather Coming Up.'

P69. Posted as Missing

Pall Mall magazine September 1906.

The Lutine Bell sounds at Lloyd's as the quill pen is dipped and moves yet again to record those words dreaded by marine underwriters and feared by seafarers' wives and families, *Posted as Missing*. Sadly, in the sailing ship era of the 18th and 19th centuries, these words would appear all too often in *Lloyd's List*, offering little hope and seldom followed by the good news all prayed for. Shoesmith, in his ten years at sea, would have witnessed all its moods, and captures here the eternal struggle of hope over expectation. The small boat, riding to a makeshift sea anchor and being tossed like a cork, is being kept head to wind and waves by the sailor who uses an oar to steer. Without the benefit of a modern emergency position-indicating radio beacon, (EPIRB) the chances of rescue in these circumstances would be remote. Not having the luxury of the yet-to-be invented radio, this sailor's ship could not have sent out a Mayday or SOS message, and reliance would thus be on the twin but slim chances of making a landfall or being sighted by a passing ship. What chance of the latter? Even from a short distance, as the boat disappeared from view in a trough and her white hull blended into the foam-topped crests, it would take the keenest of eyes and the utmost good fortune to be spotted.

P71. Spanish Waters

There are several versions of this poem, the earliest of which appeared in 1903. The version here is from Collected Poems, London, Heinemann 1931.

The gold referred to in Verse 3 was, according to an earlier version, 'won with L'Ollanais'. Real name Jean-David Nau, Francois L'Ollanais was a French-born pirate and buccaneer of the Caribbean in the 1660s, and nicknamed The Flail of the Spanish for his gratuitous cruelty.

The painting is one of four Shoesmith originals in my possession. The image was used by Anchor Line to advertise their passenger service between Glasgow and Liverpool to the USA and Canada. As that Line's headquarters were in Glasgow, it was no surprise for me to find the original painting for sale, via an internet search, with an art dealer in Scotland.

P73. The Galley-Rowers

The Collected Poems of John Masefield.

Another Masefield poem with a harking back perhaps to his *Conway* rowing days. It is, I am sure, unnecessary for me to point out to the vast majority of readers that where the poet speaks of 'grunting in the banks', he refers to banks or rows of oars rather than the edges of a river or worse, financial institutions. Shoesmith has used as a backdrop to this painting of a Viking longship, a Norwegian fjord, a scene familiar to him and often portrayed in his RMSPCo cruise posters.

P75. Ships (A)

English Review June 1912.

Masefield speaks in this poem of 'The beauty of the ships of that my city' and, knowing he was born in the Herefordshire town of Ledbury, we might ask to which city he here lays claim. The answer, given away by his reference in the second verse to St Nicholas' bells, is Liverpool, his adopted city. This was born of the formative years he spent in *Conway* when she was moored in the River Mersey, almost on the city's doorstep, the Pier Head. Familiar to him then would have been the sight of the tower of Our Lady and St Nicholas Church, *(below, the top of St Nicholas' spire)* completed in 1815 and, for many years, the tallest building in Liverpool. The church still stands today, well known to generations of seafarers as the Sailors' Church, and to locals as St Nick's. Also familiar to Masefield in his cadet days would have been the imposing waterfront edifice of the Customs House, completed in 1839 and destroyed by German bombs during World War II. It would not be until quite some years after Masefield left *Conway* that he might admire the Three Graces, the Liver Building, the Cunard Building and the Mersey Docks & Harbour Board Building, completed 1911, 1917 and 1907 respectively. The picture represents the transition years that saw steam supplant sail as the ship's driving force. The new overtakes the old and, in time-honoured fashion, hoists the courtesy signal, 'Wishing you a pleasant voyage'.

P77. Ships (B)

While the three verses of this poem, featured on the previous page, speak of the old sailing ships, 'those proud ones swaying home', Masefield's lines here bring us up to date with 'Familiar steamers' and in particular 'The Alfred Holt's blue smoke-stack'. Having a blue-painted funnel, it was inevitable that such ships of Holt's Blue Funnel Line should be referred to on Merseyside and beyond as 'Blue Flue ships', a possessive rather than derogatory term. This magnificent oil painting resides in the Ulster Museum's archive storage facility with so much of his other work, sadly hidden from public view. In fairness to the National Museums of Northern Ireland, it did feature in their six month-long exhibition of Shoesmith's work in Belfast in 2013. It is a shame that no space can be found for it on the wall of one of our many maritime museums. The picture recalls a time when British ships carried British exports to the world and imports from her Commonwealth and other important trading partners around the globe. It shows how cargo moved before containerisation, in cases, crates and cartons, in bags, barrels and bales. As a retired marine cargo insurance underwriter, I wholeheartedly endorse containerisation but the old method of 'hand-balling' as a means of loading and unloading cargo should not be forgotten. It was part of a seafarer's stock in trade as much as furling and reefing sails. Masefield did not forget. 'I come to grips.' he said, 'with half their purpose thinking of these ships.'

P79. Trade Winds

The Outlook October 1901 and subsequently in *Salt-Water Ballads.*

Being unable to find a Shoesmith scene depicting Spanish seas, tiny white houses and orange trees, all in one painting, to match Masefield's words in this poem, I selected one that features many shades of orange, *The Flower Market.* This beautiful oil painting is another of those of his that resides in the archive storage of the Ulster Museum, Belfast. It made a brief appearance at the Shoesmith Exhibition in Belfast in 2013, when the vivid colours, glowing like fiery embers almost leapt off the canvas.

P81. *Number 534*

First published in *The Times* on 25th September 1934.

The Clydebank shipyard of John Brown & Co., allocated Yard No 534 to the liner built there for Cunard White Star Line, and launched the day after the poem was published. The ship was named *Queen Mary* and the poem was included in the official launch programme. She sailed on her maiden voyage to New York on 27th May 1936 to begin a sea-going career that lasted until her sale to the city of Long Beach, California in 1967. Today, at the grand old age of 87, she is still afloat there as a hotel and visitor attraction centre, although urgently requiring a reported US$300 million to be spent on vital structural work to keep her from the breaker's torch. What of Masefield's wish that the evils of the sea,

listed in the last verse of this poem, be kept from the ship? Sadly a collision did take place on 2nd October 1942 when *Queen Mary*, on one of her many wartime crossings of the North Atlantic, sliced through her escort ship. The unfortunate ship, HMS *Curacoa* (D41) sank with the loss of 337 men from her crew of 438. Shoesmith was one of the many leading British artists and designers of the day commissioned to provide artworks for the interior of this great ocean liner, the majority being still on board and available to public view. This mural, Madonna of the Tall Ships, is one of several large works Shoesmith painted in his studio with the aid of a tall ladder, for the *Queen Mary*, and was displayed in her Second Class (Tourist) Library.

It is my hope that my book, *Cargoes*, will inspire not only further reading but also writing and painting. Not necessarily writing and painting in the styles of Masefield and Shoesmith, but certainly reflecting their respect for the sea and for the seafarers who daily face her dangers, or as the hymnist, William Whiting had it, 'those in peril on the sea'.

Acknowledgements & Bibliography

Often we read in this section of a book the words, 'Without the help of my wife, this book could not have been written.' This book is no exception and I can safely say that, without the help of my wife, Ruth, this book could not have been written.

After a long and unsuccessful search for a publisher, I found one where I should perhaps have looked in the first place. With the book centred on two former *Conway* cadets, who better to approach than the publisher of *The Cadet* magazine, the organ of The Conway Club. In Penny Reeves of Saron Publishers, I was grateful to find someone who readily espoused my dream to bring Masefield and Shoesmith back to the public recognition they deserve.

The next hurdle concerned funding, and into the breach, again through the *Conway* connection, stepped Matt Burrow who made the publication of this book a reality.

Captain Richard Woodman LVO, Elder Brother of Trinity House, for writing the foreword in his usual erudite style.

The Literary Estate of John Masefield and the Society of Authors for their kind permission to quote so much of Masefield's work.

Alfie Windsor, fount of knowledge on all things *Conway,* for advice and encouragement.

The Ulster Museum, Belfast, part of the National Museums of Northern Ireland, whose Shoesmith Collection has proved a valuable source of picture images.

Bernard Levine of Eugene, Oregon for picture images.

Dr Robert Bruce-Chwatt for picture images.

Dan at Advantec, Tenterden, for *gratis* Photoshop image.

David Watson of the Seven Seas Club for material from the Club archives.

Gervald Frykman (Warwick School Archivist) for extracts from *Warwick School: A History* by GN Frykman and EJ Hadley (Gresham Books, 2004)

Bibliography

The Collected Poems of John Masefield. Published by William Heinemann Ltd 1931

The Conway from her Foundation to the Present Day by John Masefield. Published by William Heinemann 1933

HMS Conway 1859–1974 by Alfie Windsor. Published by Witherby Seamanship International Ltd. 2008

The Wanderer of Liverpool by John Masefield. Published by William Heinemann 1930

Victorious Troy or the Hurrying Angel by John Masefield. Published by William Heinemann 1935

The Bird of Dawning or The Fortune of the Sea by John Masefield. Published by the National Maritime Museum 2009

Spunyarn Sea Poetry and Prose of John Masefield. Edited by Philip W Errington. Published by Penguin Books 2011

Sea Fever. Selected Poems of John Masefield. Edited by Philip W Errington. Published by Carcanet Press Limited 2005

Cadet became Master Writer. Article written by Trevor Boult. Published in *Telegraph Nautilus* Oct 2010

The Maritime Art of Kenneth D Shoesmith by Glyn L Evans. Published by Silver Link Publishing Limited 2010.